the golden years are a crock

To Marilyn

Richard F Carter

" Happy 50 th "

the golden years are a crock

By Richard F. Carter

Cartoons By Calvin Grondahl

LIVING FOSSIL PUBLISHING
691 PERSHING DRIVE
WALNUT CREEK, CA 9459

1ST PRINTING 1984
2ST PRINTING 1987
3RD PRINTING 1990
4TH PRINTING 1994
5TH PRINTING 1996

"The Golden Years Are A Crock"

LIVING FOSSIL PUBLISHING
691 PERSHING DRIVE
WALNUT CREEK, CA 94596

Cartoons by Calvin Grondahl
Printed in U.S.A.

ISBN-9628279-0-8
Library of Congress Catalog Card Number: 90-092317

*This book is
dedicated to all my
dead and dying
friends . . .*

1

TABLE OF CONTENTS

ABOUT THE AUTHOR

After an illustrious career as a staff artist at the Deseret News (he won the prestigious Mark E. Peterson Award in 1971 for excellence in trash maps), the multi-faceted Richard Fielding Carter has turned his talents to writing–and the world will never be the same.

Born in Salt Lake City, just in time to catch the Great Depression, he had a happy-go-lucky childhood, being shunted about among relatives, wearing hand-me-down clothes and trying to get enough to eat. He was a co-pilot on a B-24, in the U.S. Air Corps. during World War II and spent ten pleasant months as a prisoner of war in Germany. With this background, he has become an ardent supporter of the Christmas season, the military, high interest rates, taxes and religion. Although often short of facts, he readily makes up his own and has held listeners spellbound with his illuminating explanation of parity.

He has lent his piquant wit to articles on his experience as a successful gardener, a Little League baseball manager, a horseman, a raiser of neurotic dogs, and a Christmas he remembers best, particularly the heart-warming tale of the kid who dropped his new skates through a hole in the ice the first time he went to the pond to use them.

But these were pale preliminaries to his masterwork, "The Golden Years Are A Crock . . ." Mr. Carter believes that the retirement years are truly the best time of life and he bolsters this opinion with glowing instances of memorable moments in the goddam later years of oldsters, the next to last tragedy.

In view of the wide acclaim he has received in rejection slips from countless editors, agents, critics and a few illiterate winos, Mr. Carter is already at work on his next book, "The Joy of Humiliation."

What the critics say about "The Golden Years Are A Crock . . ."

"This book is offensive to all age groups."
—Viking Press

"There are some things even WE won't publish.
—Vanity Press

"I should have charged $1000, instead of $40, to read the damn thing."
—Herbert Rolfe,
Literary Agent

"The bastard's got us pegged."
—Dr. Milton Ramsay, M.D.

INTRODUCTION

Every book has a title and a message. The message of this book is so urgent that I cannot wait until a real author writes it—so I will. I have been able to condense both the title and the message into a single line of only six words, "The Golden Years are a Crock."

Most older people know these words are true, and just knowing there are millions who are sharing this experience will be of tremendous help.

So if you are planning to get old, or actually anyone who is alive and can read, this book is a must. There is some unwelcome information included in this book, but certainly by now you should be able to handle some truth. The subject of aging will be dealt with in some detail as it affects everyone, especially those who live a long time.

This book is short, as a lot of older people don't have time to read a long book, and many of us have difficulty just staying awake. Aside from that, it gave me something to do. Should anyone be inclined to read beyond the title, it will certainly do less damage than smoking, drinking, fighting or watching TV.

PASSING 55

Don't Look Back

If you are young you may grow old, or if you are old and just want to stay that way, pay attention, because this book is written about you. No one can begin too soon to plan for the next-to-last calamity, old age. You may not notice at this time, but later as you look back, you can make this observation: After 55 very few things improve physically, economically, intellectually, domestically, professionally or sexually.

It's possible, after 55 years of broken dreams, frustration, disappointments, cataclysms and some minor problems, you may have become a little cynical. Unfortunately, the next 10 or 20 years may not get any better so change your attitude, keep your expectation low and you might squeak through.

Your job could be in jeopardy, so be on guard against complacency, and don't panic. There are laws that now protect you from being fired due to age. However, you can be fired for a hundred other reasons, such as incompetence, deafness, loss of bladder control, bad eyes, senility, lascivious leering or other major infractions, all caused by age.

When you start getting old is a good time to sit down and give some thought to the real future. Here are some of the choices.

> 1. Go to Iran
> 2. Get a dangerous job
> 3. Go to New York
> 4. Go to bed and stay there
> 5. Go to Detroit
> 6. Join a monastery or convent
> 7. Commit suicide

There are many equally fine alternatives, but should you choose not to take them, here are some facts which will interest you: A large percentage of those retiring will spend their remaining years in abject poverty. A small percentage will live in moderately good circumstances, having either rich children or some criminal enterprise that they can continue to run. An even smaller percentage will live as they have lived all their lives, having amassed or inherited a fortune so great that even inflation, depression, drunkennness, dope addiction, affairs, and divorces cannot dissipate it. All of the above points should be seriously considered in making your future decisions. Will it be embezzlement or the rest home?

After retirement, the breadwinners often feel their usefulness is ended. A man can feel quite out-of-place and a little humiliated at his failures, while a woman does not necessarily feel that way. In fact, she may feel heroic for having stayed with the clown all these years while he stumbled along. She, of course, seldom neglected to show where he went wrong and even offered her help by pointing out the many things she didn't have that everyone else did. If he still has an ego after all of this, he obviously was not paying attention or was an insensitive clod and will probably outlive his wife.

On the other hand, most men have been able to amass enough guilt and anxiety to assure a constant blood pressure of 240/120. Smashing the fender of the car, cutting off a sprinkler head with the mower, the slamming of a door, a phone call at 3:00 a.m. or a thousand other minor happenings, and another instant widow is created! These are some of the reasons why many women live longer than men.

Life is really just an endurance contest and it's hard to tell the winners from the losers.

THE GOLDEN YEARS

Retirement and On Your Own

Do not believe anything you have heard about the golden years. Most of us have been conditioned from the cradle to believe that old people experience true fulfillment, a wonderful sense of accomplishment and happiness after having raised a family and lived through 45 years of work and sacrifice. This is, of course, nothing more than fraudulent propaganda.

Millions have spent their lives scrimping and saving for the great day when they can retire and spend their remaining years in leisure and the joyful pursuit of happiness, doing what they always wanted to do. Forget it! First, you're too old for that nonsense, and arthritis and inflation have ruined all your other chances.

Second, there are thousands of parasites and vultures out there waiting for you: insurance companies, whose existence depends on scaring you into buying all their supplemental insurance and never collecting; religious organizations that will promise you anything in the hereafter if you will but sign over your worldly goods in the here and now; rest homes and retirement villas; doctors, chiropractors, muggers, salesmen and second and third cousins.

So, as we face the golden years, we probably have at least one life-threatening condition, which could be a physical ailment, a psychotic spouse, resentful children, the neighbor's dog or a loose blade on the rotary lawn mower.

You have now reached that final plateau, your umbilical cord finally cut, and then the realization comes, you can only depend on yourself! A careful look at your past record will show you the serious trouble you're in!

You've just gotten your handshake or hug, a watch or jewelry, a plaque and a meager retirement stipend. They'll say, "We won't know how the hell to get along without you," but two weeks from now it will be, "Remember old what's-his-face?"

Immediately upon retirement, as one of their goals, many people want to change their lifestyles. Probably the worst thing you can do is to begin changing your old habits. To start depriving yourself of all the things you really enjoyed is the worst kind of insanity and could also add another five or ten years to your life! Always remember, sedentary people probably live longer, and therefore suffer longer.

About 48 hours after retirement, serious doubt will enter your mind as to whether or not you did the right thing. Accurate statistics are obviously not available; but, generally speaking, about 98% secretly wish they were still on the job. The other 2% were either appointed to some lucrative government position or became an executive in a prestigious charitable foundation at $200,000 per year. If you are not one of the 2%, don't dwell on the past, the present or the future, because this is unrewarding and could even lead to serious personal image and emotional problems.

It may be helpful to get into a meaningful activity, like blowing up balloons for other old people at the rest home. However, this very important kind of work is generally without remuneration. Another very popular voluntary program is surrogate grandparenting, although it's hard to understand why. One elderly man wound up with a broken jaw and bent dental plates while tucking a 19-year-old surrogate granddaughter into bed. An 87-year-old lady is still in traction after visiting 7-year-old twins and taking them for a walk in the park. The police first thought she had been mugged, but after an investigation found she had only been playing with the twins on a jungle gym.

Each retiree will have to decide how to fill his or her leisure time, but there is one universal don't–don't go back to the office right away! You may find they didn't even fill your former position, but merely moved your desk into the basement storage and you have now become what is referred to as attrition. It is almost equally disturbing to see the office-boy or janitor handling your job on his lunch hour. After several years, or perhaps just a few months, you will have forgotten what job you had and they will have forgotten who you are or where they put your desk.

It's very difficult to find anything older people are allowed to do. If it's fun, someone young is already doing it; if it's difficult, they won't let you do it anyway. However, one of the benefits is you have plenty of time on your hands to try and think of something. For instance, watch the late, late, late show on TV, since you will be awake anyway worrying about whether or not you did the right thing when you retired. There's not much reason to go to bed in the golden years if you can't sleep.

Congratulations! After 30 or 40 years of work, you have now achieved one of your most important lifetime goals and can do everything you wanted.

You may find that the first thing you must do is get a part-time job so you can eat.

FAMILY

The Real Enemy

By now you have probably realized the most disastrous result of marriage was not the possibility of murder or mayhem, but of offspring. Your reward for parenting is often demands and hostility, which should give you a clue as to what faces you in the golden years from your children. They will be either married, still living at home or both. They will also be having babies, which do not inherently bring peace of mind or endless joy. What they do bring is dirty diapers, economic problems, sleepless nights, family fistfights and divorce. There is no way you can avoid being caught up in this maelstrom should you have made the mistake of having children.

If your children are divorced, you may get the privilege of raising or tending kids until the parents can straighten out their lives, generally in 15 years or so. Accept the fact that you will never have a life of your own and cannot have any hobbies other than repairing the damage done by your loved ones. If you should choose a hobby or craft, remember there has been only one Grandma Moses, and Michelangelo wasn't married.

Regardless of all our experiences we still believe, as we have been programmed, that our families, friends and society will provide us with irresponsible fun and frivolity in spite of our aches, pains, neurosis and poverty!

By this time we should have learned that at least one thing in the Bible is true–children should leave home and cleave unto someone else. We old folks can stand just so much cleaving.

It would be impossible to describe the complexities of family life in so short a space. Simply stated, when two people fall in love, get married, have children, plunge hopelessly into debt, and then learn to fight and blame each other, that's a family.

In America at the closing of the 20th century, blood is seldom thicker than water, but money always is! Therefore, do not depend on your loved ones to care for you when you're old. In this complex society, caring for parents seems to burden the young with a handicap which will ensure them of failure. If they have not already learned to resent you, which would be unusual, this may well be the final blow.

If the trauma of family living should overwhelm you, flee! It has always been the prerogative of the young to run away; but in these times of daily crisis, more and more of the geriatric crowd are disappearing. According to reports in national media, one of the reasons for this gray-haired exodus is a newly discovered phenomenon called parent beating.

What a shock! . . . not that children abuse their parents, but that it is news. Child abuse is unforgivable; however, parent beating is something you should expect if you raise children. After all, we taught them that to survive out there they must be aggressive, and what better victims of their aggression than two loving dolts who have nursed, pampered, clothed and sacrificed for them for 20 to 25 years?

COMPANIONSHIP

Misery Loves Company

The old adage, "Two can live as cheaply as one," is only true if you each reduce your food intake by 50%. However, many people in their later years are finding it necessary to save money by sharing rent and utilities, and thereby resorting to the kind of sinful living that they condemned when they were young.

There are good and bad features of "living in sin" which must be examined. For instance, you must be very careful to pick someone who is at about your level of senility in order to maintain some sort of communication.

Sleeping with someone can be another problem. Although it provides a chance to stay warm at night, older people very often create incredible noise while asleep. If your partner is a snorer, you may be warm but awake all night, which, of course, is better than being cold and awake all night.

Another serious problem with sleeping with an older person is they can roll over on you, and you don't have the strength to push them off. You can suffocate unless you get immediate help which is not often found in your bedroom during the night.

Be especially careful not to choose a partner with apnea,

a temporary halt of the breathing process while asleep, followed by a startled awakening. It is quite common among older people. Should this misfortune be yours or your partner's, you have some really exciting nights ahead of you, although it could be that your hearing has so deteriorated you can sleep through an artillery barrage, apnea or even a 70-year-old snoring roommate.

Living together can also give you someone to talk to, which will prevent one of the most frightening aspects of old age: loneliness. But remember, just because you are

talking doesn't mean they are listening; and, in fact, most of the time you will be talking to yourself, except that it looks better when others standing around you are also talking to themselves.

The alternative to companionship is to withdraw into a solitary world of fantasy, causing families, friends and psychiatrists grave concern. While many older people engage in trivial, mundane activities, the withdrawn may very well be involved in earth-shaking events, providing world leadership, starring on Broadway, getting even, or reliving happy memories, all in their fantasy world. It's up to the individual: boring reality or winning the Reader's Digest Sweepstakes, the Publishers Clearing House contest, a $1,000,000 Las Vegas jackpot, and the Irish Sweeptakes all in one day!

If you are a widow or widower and have been driven to the edge of insanity by loneliness or boredom, it might lead you to an even more tragic happening. You could remarry! Many people have been through this several times and still do not comprehend the nature of the disaster. Unfortunately, many still persist with the idea that if they are unhappy alone, they can find happiness with a partner.

It is utterly foolish to believe that if you are unhappy alone, you will find happiness with another unhappy person. You will just compound the misery.

REMEMBERING

Just Forget It

Some people possess a good memory. It doesn't matter whether we are born with it or we develop it, the fact is as we approach these golden years, it is one more thing we start to lose. There are a lot of books written about how to retain or improve your memory, should you wish to; but I can't remember their titles.

One recommended self-improvement technique is using word association to recall places, names, and events. For instance, always think of words closely related such as wife (nag), husband (cheap), children (trouble), money (cheat), motel (sex), dog (noise), keys (lost), and so on. It can be a great source of fun, even if it doesn't help you remember.

Some thought should be given to the idea of whether a good memory is really worthwhile. Forgetting can save you a ton of money. More importantly, you can avoid the terrible frustration and pressure caused by shopping for gifts on such occasions as Valentine's Day, Easter, Mother's Day, Father's Day, Thanksgiving, Hanukkah, Christmas, anniversaries and birthdays. In fact, for the average person there are about 150 days for which you can feel either anxiety, guilt or both for not getting someone a present.

Certainly the need to forget has occurred to you by now. Just think about the last 60 or 70 years. How much have you done that is really worth remembering? There are two blank pages, following this chapter. On one write the things you would like to remember, and on the other, the things you would like to forget. Now think back to your school days: the unzipped zipper, the broken garter, the endless humiliation. How about the last three or four wars? Now recall all those wonderful decisions you didn't make. You could have bought valuable property, houses and stocks and been rich by now.

How about marriage? You could have lived a life of adventure, irresponsibility and sexual freedom, a truly hedonistic lifestyle. If you raised children you can remember a few things you would rather forget about their past behavior: 16 years (or more) of school per kid, the principal's office, long hair, drugs, cars, dating. Now, don't you really want to forget the whole damned thing?

Anyway, here you are in your twilight years wondering what happened. You have an area of your brain that handles short-term memories and another that handles long-term memories. You should cultivate the short-term memory, very little that happens to you from here on in is going to be worth remembering very long.

When we were young we could remember almost anything, but after 65 or 70 we are lucky, or unlucky, as the case may be, to remember what happened five minutes ago. All that funny stuff you heard about how Grandma and Grandpa couldn't find their glasses is true. Our memories are gone! So what? Don't even bother looking for them.

I can't remember who, but someone said, "Remembering makes life pleasurable, but forgetting makes it possible."

things I would like to remember

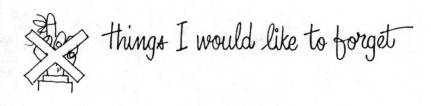 things I would like to forget

HEALTH

Still Warm and Regular

Certainly the most serious problem we old folks have is bad health, and appearance does not always tell the story. Very often, those who look the worst live the longest, or it could be the other way around. There are some very general criteria by which you can measure your health without consulting a doctor. If you feel okay, you are in good health; if you feel terrible, you are sick and should go to bed. At our age there isn't much a doctor will do except send you and Medicare a bill.

Another way of gauging health, at least for those over 70, is if they can get up at night, find the bathroom and remember how to get back to bed they are in excellent health. Those who can find the bathroom, but can't remember how to get back to bed, are only in fair health. Those who can get up by themselves, but can't remember where the bathroom is, are in poor health. Those who just lie there are in rotten health, and just don't give a damn.

If your health is good, you may live to be 100 by being careful and by keeping the same unrewarding, senseless lifestyle you have lived so far. If your health is poor, you can pay all of your life savings to the doctor and still feel rotten; but the doctor will feel good, because he now has all of your money to travel, play golf, have affairs–all of the things you should have done!

It is unfortunate that there are times when medical attention will be required, and it should be noted there are many people, including most of those on Medicare, who literally believe that Medicare and Medicaid were actually begun to help the handicapped, the old and the needy. On close examination, it should be obvious to anyone that these programs came into existence to aid the hospitals, the medical profession, the drug companies and in particular, the printing industry. Many insurance corporations were also assured of instant success, because they handle the

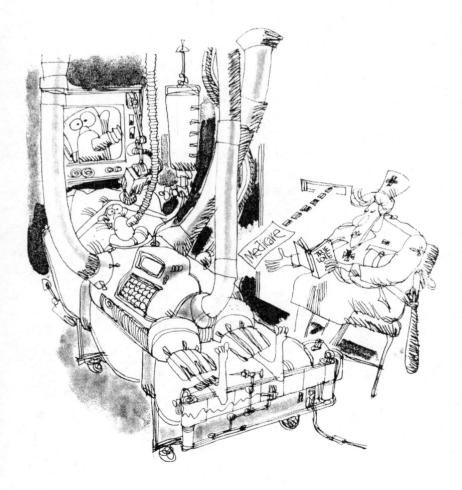

lavish flow of health care dollars from the government. It is certainly educational filling out Medicare and Medicaid insurance forms, as well as time-consuming—sometimes up to two or three weeks. Nevertheless, older Americans are grateful, even elated, that our government continues to pay these generous benefits. There is no other place in the world where old and poor people can be treated in $500 to $1,000-a-day hospital wards.

There may come a time when you are judged to be so ill you will be sent to Intensive Care. This kind of crisis will require the hospital to staff the ICU with around-the-clock personnel: 3 nurses and 19 keypunch operators to keep track of the charges and enter them into the computer. Under our high-tech medicine you may not be assured of the best medical care in the world, but you are assured of the most expensive. Some of the serious side effects of highly specialized medicine, not yet discussed in *Journal of the American Medical Association*, are bankruptcy, poverty and starvation.

In spite of everything, keeping healthy in the golden years can still be exciting, especially when trying to get the safety cap off a prescription bottle during an emergency. Some caps are more complicated than Rubik's Cube and offer a challenge of puzzle solving, eye-hand coordination, and general dexterity. Do not panic; a hammer or an axe can quickly solve the problem, should it be necessary.

So, not everything is perfect as we move into the computerized age. A more complex billing system, doctors, and hospitals can still make mistakes. For example, a 93-year-old woman living in a local rest home was having a dinner of pork chops and applesauce. She inadvertently dropped the half-eaten pork chop down her neck where it became lodged in her brassiere. She tried unsuccessfully to fish it out, and then forgot about it.

It was not located for several days until an unpleasant

odor was detected. Her doctor was called and he diagnosed it over the phone, with his home computer, as a fast-growing cancer. She was rushed to the hospital for an emergency operation. In preparing the patient for surgery, the pork chop was dislodged. The staff and doctor were amazed at the miraculous recovery from such a dread disease, and truly marvelled at the power of prayer and the ability of the human body to restore itself to health.

The pork chop was encased in plastic as an example of Porkus Mastectus Carcinoma, and a doctor bill was presented to Medicare for $6,500. The hospital bill was more reasonable, only $4,132.29 for a day-and-a-half. You can still see the 93-year-old woman occasionally looking down into her blouse and wondering what the hell happened to her pork chop.

There is also a very serious problem which exists in all surgical procedures. The older you get the more you resemble a cadaver–especially when laid out and anesthetized on an operating table. Your surgeon, preoccupied with

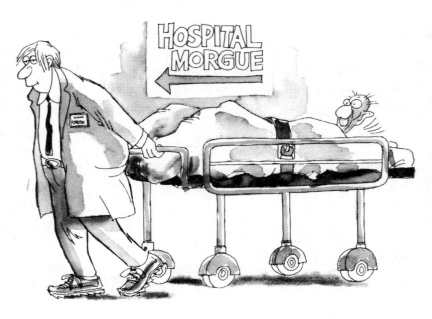

investments, Wall street, and a tension-producing affair with his surgical nurse, can easily forget it's an operation to remove gallstones, think it's a post-mortem and remove the heart or liver!

So, if you are feeling healthy by the time you reach the Golden Plateau, don't go see your doctor or go to the hospital. The risk is far too great . . . and you can't afford it anyway.

FOOD

Diet and Gas

For the old, eating has been almost as serious a problem as not eating. The reason for this is that most of us reaching 65 or older have lost our teeth, literally, and now have dentures that whistle, clack, or don't fit. Interesting statistics recently compiled on denture wearers show that 40% have somehow lost them. A further breakdown of this percentage shows that 9% of these lost dentures went down the toilet, 11% were left in restaurants under the napkin, 12% just disappeared and 8% went into the garbage in a moment of embarrassment or rage. Of the remaining 60% who hold on to their dentures, 57% are patient, long-suffering people who make the best of the problem and seem unaware of the clack, pop and whistle during their brief conversations. The remaining 3% seem to have little or no trouble, because they usually do not speak and are on intravenous feeding.

An alternative to having dentures is to get a blender, if you can afford one, which will enable you to mix up almost any distasteful food so you can drink it quickly. However, it is very important to pay attention to what you are doing. Be sure not to put your hand in the blender while it is still on, for obvious reasons, or to pour while it is still running. If you do, you will scrape your meal off the walls and ceiling.

You must remove the contents from the container, because if you should inadvertently throw in a whole can, it will make a terrible racket and could ruin your meal. Do not be too concerned if it is a cardboard carton, because there is some food value and fiber in the box itself. In addition, the glue and wax may give the food a different flavor, providing a little zing to an otherwise uneventful meal. Also remember at this time, a soft diet is better than no diet at all.

Another factor which will govern your eating as well as your living habits is the economic plight in which you find yourself. It would be silly to advise those who are wealthy, because they can eat anything they choose. However, the extremely poor will find that a great deal of time must be spent learning to fantasize. For instance, with just a little imagination a can of Bow-Wow can be a luscious meatloaf and a can of Meow served with lettuce will be a deluxe Supreme Royal Tuna Salad.

A welcome side effect of your very meager diet is that as you approach the starvation level, you will start to hallucinate. It's a fact that many less fortunate people have to pay really big money for drugs to do what you can do for nothing.

Even though your social life has now dwindled down to waving to the garbageman, you should take some pride in your dress. Very few things look worse than a tie that has been dunked in your breakfast, soaked up clam chowder from lunch and finished off with potatoes and gravy; but keep in mind that in a dire emergency, you can boil up your tie and eat it.

One unpleasant aspect of getting old is gas. Every liquid and solid food you now eat or drink, instead of turning to tissue, muscle and energy, turns to gas, making you a giant, walking explosion waiting to happen. Medical science cannot explain this phenomenon and there is no relief except the natural one.

This often requires ingenuity on your part to avoid any unnecessary embarrassment. Turn the TV on full blast, explaining to everyone present that you are hard of hearing, and in the noisy fight that ensues, you can relieve yourself. You could go outside if the weather is nice, or even if it's terrible. It is much better to be cold than the object of

outrage, scorn and pity by a roomful of people. Thirty or forty years ago, when things were more secretive, people would just go out for a "breath of air." Now, after dinner or any meal, just get up and go out. If there are young people present, they won't even know you've gone. If there are older people present, they will know damn well why you've gone.

One of the most unfortunate aspects of this problem is that as we grow older the early-warning system has gone to pot, so to speak, and it is as though the conscious part of the mind is not aware of the physical needs of the body. It does not matter whether you are standing, sitting or lying; whether you are having a chat or formal discussion. Suddenly, without warning, it happens, unmindful of the terrible embarrassment it causes you. In the event of this kind of accident, if you have a spouse just shake your head in disgust and look at him or her. However, two can play this game, so be alert! Many people have dogs for this very reason. As the foul stench fills the room, they go over and scold the dog.

A small, frail little man we knew would startle many on-lookers as he would seem to float along without touching the ground. They marveled at the miracle of levitation, but it was only *gas*!

EXERCISE

Geriatric Gymnastics

Obviously the way to avoid the medical profession and hospitals is to stay in good health. One way to do this is to not worry too much, eat properly, get the necessary amount of rest and have a balanced work and recreational program throughout your life. In other words, be born rich!

If you are not rich, then the YMCA or YWCA are able to provide you with an exercise program. Many Senior Centers also conduct classes in aerobic dancing, and the ever-popular running or jogging is economically within almost everyone's reach. It is important to choose carefully what is physically possible for you to perform. They are your muscles, your joints; and you have to live with them.

We should examine the results of physical activity by first looking at the negative aspect. It could improve your health and general outlook, causing you to live many years longer. Be realistic. If you are a rest home patient or on a fixed income, that is like hanging seven or eight more years onto your life sentence. Instead of jogging away the golden years, you could get up from a heavy meal and run the 440 at top speed. It's a more practical way of leaving the golden years behind. It will be sudden and final, making you a sure winner.

On the other hand, a more enjoyable element of exercise is watching someone else do it. This is safer, as few spectators of aerobic dancing or volleyball have coronaries. Another positive physical and intellectual exercise is to cash your Social Security check, taking it in nickels, dimes and quarters. Just carrying it home is good, heavy exercise.

Counting it and stacking it keeps your mind active and makes you feel as if you have a great deal of wealth. Also, if your relatives or a housebreaker enter your home, it will take them a long time to find and gather up all that loose change.

To summarize, exercise for the young or affluent is called recreation, but for those who have survived to the golden years, it's just a lot of work. Observe the expressions of agony seen on the faces of most of the nuts running around your town. It sure looks like a hard way to have fun.

If you find pleasure in viewing the continuing comedy, it is best to do so with your motor on idle. It gives you the most mileage.

APPEARANCE

Faking It

You may not think it makes a great deal of difference how you look to others once you have reached the golden years; but as usual, you are wrong. You can, however, get rid of your formal wear, go to the Goodwill store and purchase a chic new-old wardrobe. Careless dress, old clothes, worn-out running shoes and sweat suits somehow denote eccentric sophistication. (Be sure you don't buy the stuff you just gave away!)

This casual appearance will also help you to travel unnoticed in relative safety, as an old decrepit outfit will discourage hoodlums. Even your friends and family will cross the street, if they recognize you, believing you have finally jumped the track.

It is no longer necessary to make those urgent trips to the barber shop, even if you still have hair. In fact, some men welcome baldness. After failing to communicate with their barbers for over 50 years, they are tired of looking like an Idaho potato farmer. Most barbers are born with Alzheimer's disease anyway.

Elderly women have a tendency to experiment with tints to achieve that glamorous look the cosmetic companies promote. They risk the weird effects that sometimes result from trying to change the color of their hair. For instance, in attempting to dye their hair a lovely shade of lavender, they end up with a deep purple mop. In an effort to lighten it, their hair turns green as the Emerald Isle. Frantically they apply something else to make them look human, and they become a carrot top. Chances are by this time most of it is on the bathroom floor, so they sweep it up and plan to stay indoors until they grow a brand new head of hair.

Another more drastic method for improving your looks is cosmetic surgery. Face lifts or hair transplants will seldom return your former appearance–which probably wasn't that great anyway. Some very serious consequences can result when excess tissue accidentally returns to its former position. One poor lady had a nine pound double chin sewn up behind her ears. It suddenly broke loose while she was at a luncheon, fractured her neck, plunged into her chicken gumbo soup and ruined some honored guests' very expensive gowns.

So, keeping up appearances in the golden years is questionable, especially after you have spent hours putting yourself together and someone asks: "When are you going to get ready?"

REST HOMES

Just Hanging Around

The most desirable way to spend your golden years is avoiding rest homes. They are a little like zoos, although not as much fun to visit. The inhabitants are no longer dangerous, but they spend their days with little else to do but pace and roam the halls, waiting for food, visitors or sleep.

The one thing rest homes offer is time. They get you up early so you can spend as many waking hours as possible pondering your fate. Gradually your senses will dull and you will require less and less attention. However, your payments will not be less and less, but rather more and more. Unfortunately, there is little chance of escape from the rest home once you have arrived, but you can immediately join in the excitement of sitting around waiting for yourself or your roomie to expire.

Generally, rest homes have an entertainment hour. This consists of dragging all the old people out of their rooms into a central location, where for one solid hour they are forced to watch or listen to probably the worst talent ever assembled. They may be urged to throw plastic balls to one another to the tune of "Silver Threads Among the Gold," or to dance with one of the keepers to a fast 1927 fox trot, played by three practicing alcoholics using a piano, a washtub and a fiddle. Some of the more fortunate ones lapse into a protective coma, while others remain conscious throughout.

If you protest you can't see or don't want to dance, they won't listen, because they can't understand that you are 97 years old and don't want to play. It's not true that you are a poor sport, you just don't want to do it. One way to discourage involvement is to throw up on them. They will then leave you alone.

The best kind of entertainment is that which is unplanned. If you are one of those who can still laugh at yourself, you will be privileged to watch some of the greatest comedy on earth. A rest home is slapstick at its finest. You must simply be the audience, not a participant. Mealtimes provide the best laughs. However, not an hour passes from getting up, trips to the restroom (wrong one) and going to bed (wrong room), that some little tragicomedy isn't enacted.

One rest home resident, a former ballet dancer, organized a ballet company of patients over 75. The purpose was not to gain national recognition, but to send the participants out of this world actively pursuing a goal. It was unfortunate that it did not really get off the ground, but during the several weeks of practice it provided some truly great entertainment. Visualize a troupe of geriatrics doing "Swan Lake." After the first curtain at least half the cast was in shock or cardiac arrest. The only survivors were those who couldn't learn their parts and just wandered around the stage dressed up like large ducks. There were only a few rehearsals, because the 87-year-old ballerina kept running out of dancers, and that really was the purpose. She is now waiting for new members.

Boredom at rest homes is one of your greatest assets. It prevents you from becoming involved in any worthwhile activities. If you have learned anything at all in your lifetime, you must know that doing something worthwhile is accompanied by frustration and disappointment. So it boils down to a rather easy choice, shall I be bored or frustrated? Frustration causes anxiety and high blood pressure, boredom causes sleep.

The alternatives are to plan early for an independent future or to buy your own rest home. Remember, you can't trust friends, relatives, banks, churches or the government. You could invest all of your money in a trust administered by your dog or cat, who will have to support you for the rest of your days. They may not be great administrators, but can be trusted more than bankers and lawyers.

Before government got involved in providing for the aged, families had the responsibility for their care. Billions of dollars have been spent (enough to build luxury apartments for everyone over 40), but all we have are expensive warehouses called rest homes. If, in an attempt to alleviate crowding, oldsters were allowed the choice of a penthouse at the Waldorf Astoria or a rest home, the expense would be the same. One governmental recommendation was to raise the Titanic, refurbish it and make apartments of the staterooms for the elderly. No action has yet been taken, nor have there been any appropriations made. It has even been suggested that we are already on it.

The irony is that most old people are still waiting for their ship to come up.

SEX AFTER SEVENTY

Fantasy Land

If sex was a problem at 16 or 17, it will probably still be one at 70. If you are the victim of a normal marriage and were married to the same woman for 45 years or more, she said no nine times more often than she said yes. You may find that now when she says no, you don't care or, in fact, are relieved. If you are still interested, she will have found other excuses, unless you are so dumb you still believe the old ones.

If you are a woman and have been married to the same man for 45 years or more, it's incredible that you only said no as often as you did. It generally won't take much to discourage him in these golden years. His attention span has been reduced to four or five seconds, so simply change the subject and he will have forgotten what it was he wanted.

A survey was taken some time ago of 100 elderly people, to show on a scale of 1 to 10 what the most important things were in their golden years. Only 2 of the 100 mentioned sex in the top 10, and they each mentioned it ten times from their padded cells. It might interest you to know what the 10 choices were: (1) going to the toilet, (2) eating, (3) watching TV, (4) going to bed and (5) being warm. The other five were divided among pets, fire engine sirens, balloons, Sesame Street and Dr. Seuss.

One of the dangers of sex in these late years is the "Sexual Coronary." If you still have the ability to perform, it could lead to the big one (heart attack). It doesn't happen often, but an orgasm and heart attack at the same moment will surely put an end to the golden years. So do your best, it sure beats cancer or diabetes.

Much will depend on your marital status. If you are still married to the same spouse, your sex life probably ended 30 years ago. However, if you find yourself free to pursue sexual engagements (pursue is the wrong word for those over 70), be certain that you let him or her do all the work. It is very important now, whenever the urge strikes, not to hesitate. That old saying, "Each time may be your last," is now literally true.

If you and your partner are of similar age it is best to wait until dark, for obvious reasons. In the early years of marriage or as an adult prior to the golden years, physical appearance was often sufficient to spark a sexual encounter. Things are different now; you should remember that you may look very much like a circus sideshow team. You must fantasize, especially during daylight hours, otherwise sex is impossible, because it is very difficult to make love in a state of hysterical laughter.

Sex is also difficult if you should have severe arthritis or rheumatism. The mind is only capable of concentrating on one thing at a time, so do not think of the pain of arthritis, but dwell on the joy of sex.

Unless you are very fortunate in these golden years, sex is just another three letter word. It should be obvious why SEX AFTER SEVENTY is such a short chapter; what's to write about?

JUNK MAIL

Cheap Entertainment

Nearly everyone complains about getting junk mail. During the golden years this may be the only communication many of us will have with the outside world. Children relatives, and friends are so engrossed in their own survival that they don't often drop by. Most of your friends are so old they can't remember where they live, let alone where you live, or even who you are.

Remember, the postman comes by every day, so get on everyone's mailing list. Just buy one thing through the mail or give $5 to a charity and the deluge will begin. There is no further cost. One old guy got 140 pounds of mail in one day, but the average is only about 6 or 7 pounds. He is now three years behind in reading his junk mail, even though he is a fast reader! He also pays the first month's premium on all the insurance brochures that solicit him as a customer. Sometimes it is only 10 or 25 cents, and he is either turned down or drops the policy. In any given month he has three or four hundred thousand dollars worth of life and health insurance, and plenty of mail. However, there is no record of any insurance company paying benefits from that kind of offer.

Another facet of junk mail is the giant giveaway contest. Enter all of them, even though the chances of winning are almost nonexistent. Every day you can look forward to winning; this will keep your hopes high. Remember, someone has to win. There was an 85-year-old woman who won $500,000. She was courted by and fell in love with a 29-year-old man. Naturally, with such an age difference, they had little in common, so he encouraged her to take up rock climbing. It was a disastrous choice for her, as she did it only once. So even when you win, you lose.

You don't have to buy the products or magazines, so be careful to read the nine pages of instructions and paste the yes or no stamp in the proper place. Accidentally subscribing to unwanted magazines, books or a set of encyclopedias at this time of life does not enhance the golden years.

Advertising brochures can provide great reading as long as you don't believe them or buy anything. Don't feel obligated or guilty just because they were addressed to you, the Resident. There are also coupons which often come in the mail and are generally thrown out. One little 94-year-old lady collects them from the neighbors' garbage and anywhere else she can find them.She now has $11 million in coupons, giving a real sense of security as she can't possible spend them all. She may also wind up in the Guiness Book of World Records.

So, as you can see, there are ways to entertain yourself in the golden years. Christmas comes once a year, but junk mail knows no season

CRIME

Senior Sitting Ducks

More and more older people are finding themselves victims of crime. If you are wealthy, you are a prime target for extortion, kidnapping, robbery and murder, usually by your own family. If you are poor, you are still not safe, but remain a good mark for extortion, robbery and murder, usually by your own family. The one real advantage of being old and poor is that no one is going to kidnap you; however, you are likely to be beaten up more often.

Many wealthy people now resort to hiring bodyguards, but even in this there is some danger. Ex-police officers or former prizefighters make excellent guards, but it is critical that a thorough look at their past be conducted, as often police officers who know how profitable crime is will take a job just to find an easy mark . . . you. Prizefighters are less prone to resort to this kind of inside crime, since they generally are not very bright; but they can, if things don't go their way, resort to instant violence–not against an intruder, but against you!

Canine protectors can also be effective, and have an I.Q. similar to prizefighters, though they are a little more dependable. However, they often forget whether they are protecting your home or their own territorial prerogative. To avoid being a victim of your own dog, keep noise to a minimum when entering your property, because dogs attack those who are the loudest, which isn't likely to be the burglar or mugger. However, don't try to sneak past a sleeping dog, as they have extremely sensitive ears and are trained to react instantly to any unusual behavior, even yours. As an added precaution, it is wise to send your partner in first, or wrap both arms in blankets before entering your home after an evening out on the town.

Perhaps one of the safest methods of home protection is a recording of a snarling, barking dog, actuated by the breaking of an electrical circuit. But if you should stumble out of bed half asleep and open a window, thereby breaking the circuit, it can be quite a shock, and at your age you don't need this kind of nighttime excitement. The frightening noise of the recording has even been known to cause an

occasional cardiac arrest, not of a burglar but of the home-owner! Not everything works as planned.

Some people put up signs saying, "Beware of Dog." This effectively keeps friends and family away. A sign saying, "Salesmen and Muggers Will Be Shot" works well against everyone except salesmen and muggers!

Owning weapons may give you a real sense of security, but because the older person's reaction time is often slow, the attacker may wind up using your weapon against your mate, your mutt and you. Also, if you are not experienced in the handling of modern weapons you can point them the wrong way, knocking out your partner or even doing yourself in, leaving the attacker at liberty to go about his business with your home undefended.

For security in public, one solution is crowds, because safety in numbers is very true. Your appearance is also important. If you are a woman, wear several dresses and a coat in the middle of summer. If you are a man, do the same thing. Eccentricity discourages muggers and purse snatchers! Remember, dress worse than the people you are with, so if attack does come they will be the target. It's survival of the shabbiest!

For further protection, a man should wear a cheap watch and not carry a wallet, just a dollar and loose change so you won't be killed. A woman can carry a cheap purse or handbag, but be certain it is empty of any valuables. When it is snatched make a terrible, hysterical scene so the thief believes it contains a lifetime of savings. Then get the hell out of there, because when he finds it stuffed with old newspapers, he is going to be mad and come back looking for you.

Try to keep your money in a safe place–which is where you aren't! If you do have your money or valuables at home, hide them. This brings up the problem of forgetting where all your hiding places are. Of course, looking for them in your many leisure hours can provide entertainment.

The only place cash should be used is at the supermarket. Even here the outrageous prices charged can be described as extortion or outright robbery, but at least you get a small bag of groceries to carry out.

It's unbelievable that someone reaching the golden years would trust anybody. Surprisingly enough, though, a common crime to which most old people are susceptible is the con game. To avoid ever being a victim of this game, never give cash to strangers, politicians, firemen, churches, charitable groups, friends, distant relatives or immediate family. Be wary even if they identify themselves as FBI agents or bankers trying to catch a crooked teller. There are very few dishonest tellers, but you should know by now that neither the FBI nor bankers can be trusted.

If you do become the victim of a crime, just be glad that at your age you still have something that someone else wants.

TRANSPORTATION

You Can't Get There From Here

Getting around is difficult, as is everything else attached to the golden years. If you don't like to go out, it will seem that people are constantly dragging you out in spite of your protests. If you do want to go out, you will find that in a nation of 300 million cars, buses and motorcycles, it will take a week of careful planning to get a ride to the supermarket.

One way is to dial 911 and complain of chest pains and smelling smoke. When the ambulance and fire engine arrive, just ask one of them to drop you off at the supermarket, explaining that the pain has gone away. Do not use this method to get home.

When finished shopping, act befuddled. Explain to the clerk or manager that you've forgotten where you parked your car, you don't know where you live or any other reasonable excuse. He will then call the police to get rid of you. When you are comfortably seated in the police car, conveniently remember who you are and where you live. They will either beat you up, take you home or both. Don't do this too often, but with a little imagination and improvisation you can bring some excitement into your life and get to and from the places you want to go.

There are, of course, other forms of transportation. Buses are the most common and cheapest, although you should be sure-footed before risking this. A hostile or new driver with a quick start or stop can put you in traction for the rest of your life. One way to avoid falling is to crawl on and off on all fours, creating sympathy but seldom bringing help. Jogging or hitchhiking can be an invitation to assault or robbery, so these are not recommended. Taking a taxi could cost you half of your Social Security check. You could steal a car, if you can still drive, but the result might be five to ten years.

If all else fails, ask one of your kids to please spare an hour or so. This is usually the most difficult of all.

DEPRESSION

It Can't Last Long

Depression usually begins early and its root cause is a poor self-image, so most people have learned to be depressed by the time they are 21. If, of course, you haven't learned by 65, you have not been paying attention to what's happening around you.

Those who love us most usually spend their lives helping us recognize our faults and shortcomings. If they should fail, most of us will reinforce their observations by our own actions. The cumulative effect of having a spouse and raising children from infancy through the teens and their eventual marriages, children, grandchildren and divorces is the classic blueprint for lifetime depression.

Unless you were chairman of the board, governor, senator, or the godfather, it is best not to dwell too much on the past, because there probably isn't enough time left to cure a deep depression caused by reflection on a lifetime of failures. As you will see, there are many successful ways of eliminating depression. One of the most popular is suicide. This, of course, is a rather severe measure, but certainly the way to avoid recurring bouts. Also, society will benefit if you are a welfare recipient. If you are wealthy, you are probably bananas, and society loses another nut! In either case, this selfless act will always be misunderstood.

Hospitalization is also frequently used to deal with depressed senior citizens. It is far and away the most lucrative solution for the hospitals and the medical profession, because in many cases they are able to keep the patient depressed for several months. Upon being released, it is wise not to look at the bill. Very often when patients examine the charges and realize they could have bought a home, a new car and left an inheritance for their families with the money paid to hospitals and psychiatrists, they become even more deeply depressed. They may even suffer a fatal stroke or heart attack, either of which is also a final cure.

Another recommended therapy for depression is to establish some short term goals—very short. Decide on some things you want to do, then eliminate those things you can't do because of physical or economic restrictions. The choice will now be very small, which could be extremely depressing in itself; so maybe TV, fantasy and sleep will be your only alternatives.

From all of this we can conclude that the only sure cure for depression is an early demise. Failing that, physical or intellectual activity is the cheapest way to lessen depression, but at our age probably neither is possible.

RETIREMENT VILLAS

Living It Up

Much to their dismay even the rich get old, though they have always felt that this honor and distinction should go to the poor. However, those with sufficient money to keep them in luxury or near luxury will find that growing old "ain't all that bad."

For the fortunate few, retirement communities are now very popular, promising a life of exclusivity and activity. These wealthy colonies often use very sophisticated and romantic names like Villas, Estates, and Manors; but it is always wise to investigate before making a very substantial investment. For example, Ocean View Villa in Oklahoma, Monte Carlo Manor in Detroit, or Mountain View Estates in Nebraska should cause suspicion. Remember, there are no refunds, and once situated, very few residents ever willingly move, though they do depart at a sometimes alarming rate.

One drawback to this kind of living is that people tend to be cliquish. To be accepted as part of the clique will require some changes in your lifestyle; but once you are accepted, the dizzying pace of fun and entertainment will be as tough as being a migrant farm worker and the hours will be almost as long.

At 9:00 a.m. you and your spouse will fall out for a breakfast of Bloody Marys at Mr. and Mrs. Torkelson's. At 10:07 it's golf, after having made a very quick change from early morning cocktail elegance to high fashion golf togs. After driving a cart an exhilarating 18 holes, shooting 127 and 170 respectively, and laughing about whiffs and missed seven-inch putts, you are ready to collapse. However, at 4:00 p.m. sharp you must be at the Van der Smythe's for the afternoon "happy hour," after which you have 53 minutes to shower, change, nap and be off to a formal

dinner at the Panelli's, followed by cocktails with the Goldbergs at 11:00 p.m. It's hard having this much fun every day!

Golf, cocktail parties, endless brunches and dinners will occasionally be interrupted by group excursions to cultural events such as the opera, symphony and gala charity functions. This leaves you little time to worry about the rapid deterioration of your body or the world.

Unfortunately, the world hasn't changed, and crime and violence can be found even in these wealthy retirement communities. In one instance, several strollers near the shimmering reflection pool were visibly shaken when they witnessed Arthur Livingston Marshall IV yelling, "Stop, thief!" while chasing a woman with a duck in her arms. The authorities finally restored order, after explaining that the ducks belong to everyone, and the woman was Mr. Marshall's wife.

Retirement communities offer many things, and certainly an end to loneliness, as residents euphorically lock-step their way through the golden years.

SOME FINAL THOUGHTS

My message in all of this is that without a sense of humor there is no point in reaching the golden years. This can be the funniest time of life if you just take a look at yourself and realize that all those crises were really not that important. After all, there are some good things that do come about, even in old age. The trick is to recognize them.

If you are a woman, you will no longer have to tolerate the "leering machos," the suggestive remarks from big mouth juveniles. If you are a man, no one expects much from you. Your lustful attitudes have been reduced to almost nothing, so you and those around you can now relax. Assuming you still entertain some sexual fantasies about a young woman, few, if any, entertain any fantasies about you. If you have an old "turkey" at home, you can both fantasize or have a good laugh together.

You will discover that the love of antiques does not extend to old folks, so don't be offended when you find that a Revolutionary War musket or pioneer sideboard gets more attention than you. In this mad technological society, you will seldom receive much adulation or consideration, although you have surely earned some in a lifetime of living. Just remind your family that you can still be shown as a dependent on an IRS 1040.

It may also come as a rude awakening that most TV commercials with cheery old people, loving families and caring friends are as realistic as Saturday morning cartoons. If you are fortunate enough to have money, your life can be much like these ads, with you the star. You will be fawned over, humored, pampered and loved because, for some reason, rich old folks are more lovable than poor old folks.

You can take pride in having survived this dramatic, explosive 20th century, from the horse and buggy to interstate highways, supersonic flight, putting a man on the moon and now the beginning of the exploration of the galaxy with Pioneer II. You've lived through the great depression of the '30s, three or four wars, five or ten recessions. There will never be another show like this one. You can now remember all of your past mistakes with a certain detachment for the simple reason there isn't time to repeat them. Besides, most of your mistakes have been forgotten by everyone but you.

There isn't much you can do about the possible and ominous threat of global economic collapse, social revolution, world hunger, massive unemployment or nuclear holocaust. So relax! Let the economists, the politicians and the generals get us out of the mess they got us into.

A lot of misleading rhetoric has been used to describe the golden years, very little of it factual. Only a fool would rather be old than young. As Samuel Clemens said, "There is no sadder sight than a young pessimist, except an old optimist," and, "The man who is a pessimist before 48 knows too much; if he is an optimist after it, he knows too little."

It would seem the golden years is a misnomer. Truly the golden years are those years of youth, when life is forever, before real awareness and responsibility.

Yet growing old is an unavoidable experience if you insist on living–and there are many who never get the chance.

Old age should be the years when we can view the past with maturity, without regret, and the future with full awareness that it is short. We should have made some conscious consideration about dying, so it will not come as a fearful surprise that we are not going to live forever.

Should there be anything beyond the grave, it will be a hell of a surprise to everyone, especially the Religious nuts who have it all worked out here on Earth. Life and death are inseparable, clothed in a cloak of magnificent mystery, so don't fret it, just live like every day is your last one, because it very well might be.

Those of you who are still young, gird up your loins, whatever that means, because a very wise man said, "Old age ain't for sissies."

The Golden Years in pictures.

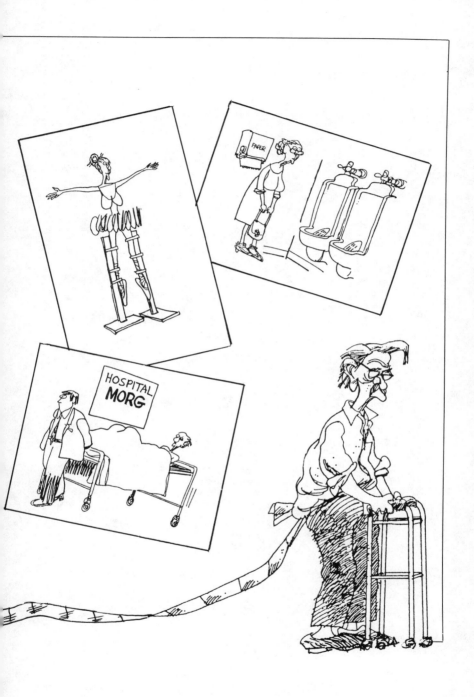

the end